A CASTLE BY THE SEA

The Whitstable Castle Story

by

J. A. FRAME

First published 2013 by J A Frame

All rights reserved. No reproduction, copy or transmission of this publication may be made without written permission. No paragraph may be reproduced, copied or transmitted save with written permission or in accordance with the provisions of the Copyright Act 1956 (as amended).

Latest Update: 19 June 2013   Number of Words: 12589

Copyright © J A Frame 2013

ISBN: 978-1-291-46066-7

Lulu.

www.lulu.com

Front Cover: Whitstable Castle today

CONTENTS

INTRODUCTION	3
THE CASTLE FAMILIES	7
THE BEGINNING IS IN THE PAST	9
THE FORGOTTEN REVOLUTION	13
PEARSON AND STEAM	17
• Pearson goes to court	21
ART AND LOVER	23
• Wynn Ellis MP	25
THE PEN IS MIGHTIER THAN THE SWORD	31
THE PLAYWRIGHT	39
THE MYSTERY OWNER	41
THE END OF AN ERA	43
• Kate Anderson	45
THE MALLANDAIN FRIEZE	47
THE BUILDING OF THE CASTLE	49
A NEW BEGINNING	55
THE GARDENS	57
• The Green Flag Award 2012	59
WHITSTABLE UDC	61
MEMORIES	63
CONCLUSION	67

INTRODUCTION

The Author

John Andrews Frame (Andrew) was born and educated in South London. He studied theology with the London Baptist Association and at Regents Park College, Oxford, and for some years has undertaken lay preaching appointments.

Andrew was employed as a quality control inspector for British Gas and he also qualified as an assistant podiatrist with the National Health Service, during which time he was co-writer of a paper on aftercare following nail surgery.

He is married with a daughter Sarah and son Stephen, who lives with his family in Canada and to whom this book is dedicated.

He moved to Whitstable in 2007 where he lives with his wife Margaret.

The Research

I took up a post as a volunteer at Whitstable Castle and, after reading 'Copperas and the Castle', by Geoffrey Pike, and other publications, it became obvious to me that there was more to tell about Whitstable Castle and the lives of the occupants.

However, after close enquiry I could find no books on the history of Whitstable Castle – there are books on the history of Whitstable but they have only a passing note on the Castle, some of which are inaccurate and based on supposition.

This book looks at the lives and times and the impact the owners had on the house, and on Whitstable, and is the result of a great deal of in-depth research.

The study of documents at various archives, and on the internet, showed a wealth of hidden information – with some surprises along the way!

The History

I believe history matters. Much of the history that we learn can be biased and distorted. This work has been an exploration, as far as possible, into the past lives of those who lived in Whitstable Castle.

I hope to inform and enlighten and this work aims to reveal a concise history of Whitstable Castle and its impact on the town. It is the result of many hours of research on the Internet and in the press, talking to people, and visiting ancestral homes, graveyards, Mausolea and other places associated with the people concerned.

To that end my thanks go out to a host of people:

The staff past and present of Whitstable Castle for their help and encouragement and for passing on their knowledge of the castle story to me; to those who let me visit the appropriate homes; to the many people I have met that have given me help in one form or another – if I were to name them all it would take a book on its own!

While much of the information has been gathered from old files and sources too numerous to record, I must acknowledge the invaluable support I have received. All of which have, in some way, made this publication possible:

The Parliamentary Archives; The staff at Canterbury Cathedral Archives; The staff at the many museum sites contacted; The Archivists at various seats of learning; Brian Thynne of the National Maritime Museum; The Staff of the KCC library service, Swalecliffe and those of numerous libraries, museums and academia; Members of staff at various graveyards and cemeteries; People I have met either in person or on the internet; Geoffrey Pike – to whom my thanks for all his help and advice; The late Robert H Goodsall FRIBA, for his early works; The National Fencing Museum; and the Mallandain Family History, Canada.

My thanks also to Patricia Blake for her artwork, and to Tony Harris for his help in producing this book.

I am not an historian, just a layman with an interest in the history, life and times of the castle on Tankerton Hill.

In his book, 'Whitstable, Seasalter and Swalecliffe', Robert H Goodsall writes:

> "Every village or hamlet in the country has its own domestic history, intimately bound up with the daily lives of the inhabitants. In many ways this is far more interesting and valuable in presenting a true picture of bygone generations than the story of larger and more spectacular events which is the duty of the general historian to chronicle."
>
> Goodsall 1938

Voltaire, the 17th century historian, wrote:

> "An historian has many duties. Allow me to remind you of two which are important. The first is not to slander; the second is not to bore."

I hope I do neither!

John Andrews Frame f.c.a.

THE CASTLE FAMILIES

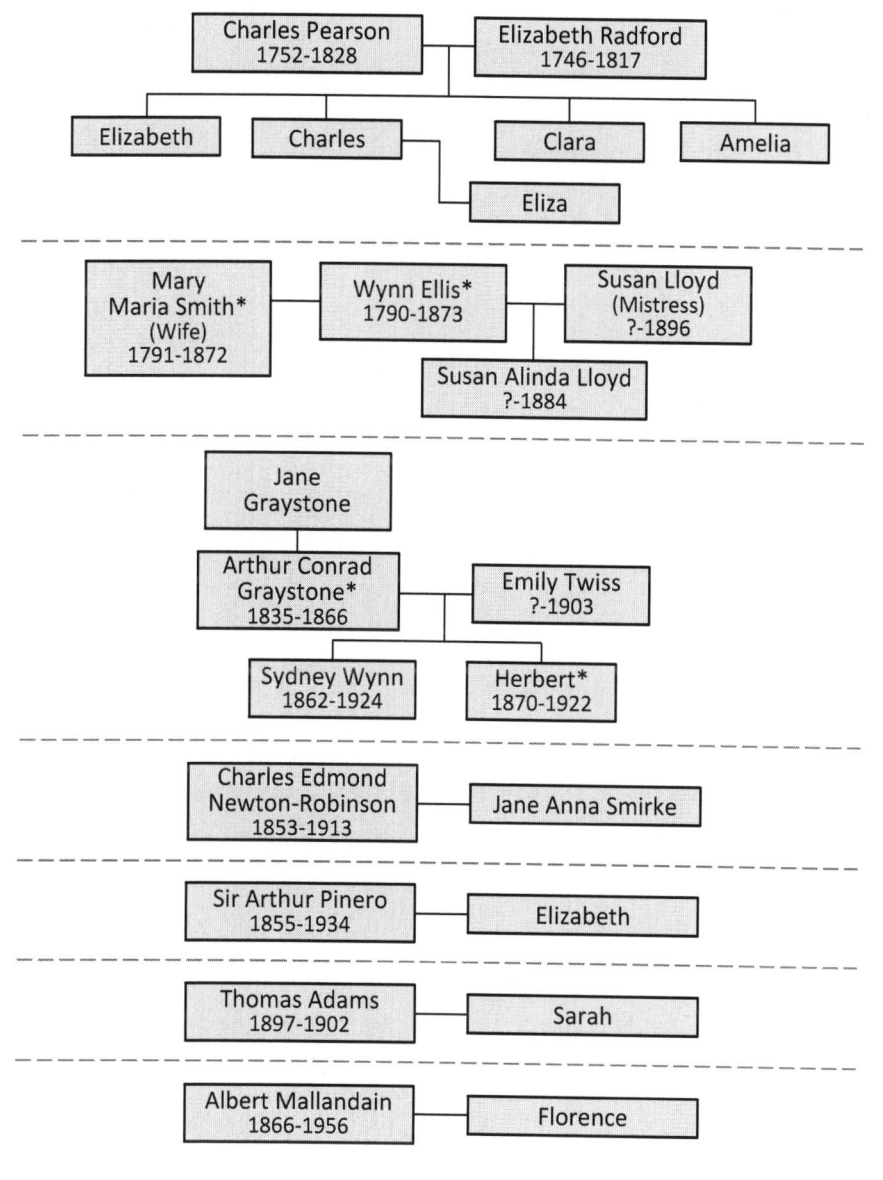

- Charles Pearson 1752-1828 — Elizabeth Radford 1746-1817
  - Elizabeth
  - Charles
  - Clara
  - Amelia
  - Eliza

- Mary Maria Smith* (Wife) 1791-1872 — Wynn Ellis* 1790-1873 — Susan Lloyd (Mistress) ?-1896
  - Susan Alinda Lloyd ?-1884

- Jane Graystone
- Arthur Conrad Graystone* 1835-1866 — Emily Twiss ?-1903
  - Sydney Wynn 1862-1924
  - Herbert* 1870-1922

- Charles Edmond Newton-Robinson 1853-1913 — Jane Anna Smirke

---

- Sir Arthur Pinero 1855-1934 — Elizabeth

- Thomas Adams 1897-1902 — Sarah

- Albert Mallandain 1866-1956 — Florence

Interned in All Saints Graveyard, Whitstable

THE BEGINNING IS IN THE PAST

Whitstable, in the south east corner of England, is 60 miles from London and seven miles from Canterbury. It once wallowed in the middle of the great land bridge that joined England to the rest of Europe.

Instead of the sea, wind farms and forts you see today, a vast shallow valley and swamp beds would have stretched out before you, home to mammoths, elks, and from time to time, migrating humans.

As the North Sea forced its way south, it created a large bay forming the estuary of the Thames and Swale. Tankerton Slopes were carved out by the ever increasing force of water and wind from the melt waters during the end of the last ice age.

The Castle as it is now known has had many names – The Manor, The Towers, Tankerton Towers and finally Whitstable Castle – the name it acquired in 1934 when it became the offices of the Whitstable Urban District Council. It was built as a home, not a castle in the true sense of being a fortified structure in the style of Dover, Rochester, Leeds and others. However, the owners still had an imposing hold over the town.

It is a building with a chequered past, linked to the industrial history and development of, not only the town, but the world.

It was after the Norman Conquest that William the Conqueror gave the manors of Whitstable, Seasalter and Swalecliffe to Bishop Odo, his half-brother who fought alongside him at the Battle of Hastings. Although Odo would not lift a sword in the battle, the Bayeux Tapestry shows him clubbing the invaders. He was given the title of Earl of Kent, and the castle at Dover.

Odo was granted manors in thirteen counties which gave him an income of over £3,000 per year, making him the richest tenant-in-chief in the kingdom.

The 'Lord of the Manor' was a term which originated in the Middle Ages. After the Battle of Hastings a feudal system was established in England by the Normans. All the land in England was claimed by William the Conqueror and distributed amongst the Normans as their reward for fighting for him.

The estates and land given were known as Manors and the Lord of the Manor owed allegiance to the King.

Whitstable is not recorded in the Doomsday Book although Nortone (Northwood), one of its three Saxon names, is.
In 1254, the son of King Edward I was knighted the Master of the Hospital at Ospringe, to the south of Faversham. He paid for half a fee of land held in Tangreton (alias Beconfield) held by knight's service within Whitstable, from Robert de Mescegros.

Hasted: Book of Roll on Knight's Fee/Charles Drake AC (Arch Cant.) XXX(43) & Madox.

The master of the Maison Dieu of Hospreng holds half a knights fee in Tangerton within Whitstable from Robert de Mescegros.

From Lists of knights fees in Kent 1256.

The Charter Rolls, the administrative record of the time, show that in 1258, William de Tangreton had 120 acres of land in Whitstable.

During the reign of Edward III (1327-1377) the land became part of the possession of the hospital, or Maison Dieu, at Ospringe.

Mike Frohnsdorff, historian at the Maison Dieu writes:

> *"It seems land at Tankerton and Whitstable was an important holding... one of the prize assets."*

It survived for more than three centuries until disbanded in 1519 on the instructions of King Henry VIII to grant all its revenues and possessions to endow St John's College, Cambridge. The Maison Dieu was a considerable landmark along the pilgrim route and for travellers to Canterbury, Dover and the Continent.

The Tankerton Land then became known as Beaconfield in Whitstable.

My understanding of the use of the land indicates that there was property on the land before. To what end and where, must still remain a mystery. (Ed.)

There is reference that Tankerton Towers stands on the site of St Ann's farm. This, however, is not so: the farm was set more to the west. This may, however, have been the farm from which they got their supplies. The farm was on the Towers' land.

THE FORGOTTEN REVOLUTION

It was in the 16th century that a Forgotten Revolution started, not with coal and iron, or by populist uprising, but in chemistry. At that time Whitstable was at the forefront of an industry that was to change the face of the world.

In the 15th century, Queen Elizabeth I ordered the search for deposits of 'alum', a mineral used mainly for fixing dyes in cloth so that the bright colours of drapes at the court or clothing did not run.

Sites were found in the cliffs at Tankerton, and the first opencast mine operation opened in 1588.

Smelting works were built where the bowling green is located, and on the site of the Castle Tea Gardens, Tower Hill.

On the slopes at Tankerton and around the Thames Estuary from the late 16th century and into the 19th, was found Copperas, a little-known chemical today, but back then one which played an important part in Britain's industrial development some 200 years before the industrial revolution.

Copperas manufacture required huge investment in plant and materials and the chemical took four years to produce. Such investment required a financial return, and profits were consequently high.

It is a mineral ore, iron pyrite, occurring naturally in the local London clay, washed out of the coasts of the Thames estuary by marine erosion in the form of thin twig-like fossils called 'copperas stones'. These are in the form of brownish spherical nodules known as marcasite, or in twig-like fossil form with brown iron staining. It also resembles petrified animal droppings.

The principal use of copperas was as a dye fixative for woollens. It was also used in the manufacture of gun powder and ink and was used in sheep dipping.

During the medieval period copperas mixed with Thornwood extract had been used as scribe's ink.

The copperas industry received a significant boost during the English Civil War (1642-51), when there was a massive increase in the demand for uniforms, gunpowder, saddles, harnesses, etc.

In Kent, the main production sites were at Whitstable, Deptford, and Queenborough on the Isle of Sheppey.

The London market took a large share of the product and the Capital played its part in the growth of the Whitstable works.

Early interest in the Whitstable copperas industry is recorded in a letter written in 1569 by the Archbishop of Canterbury, Matthew Parker, to Sir William Cecil. Referring to an unidentified 'poor man', the archbishop wrote:

> *"This poor man signifieth that by the counsel of a stranger he hath found out the making of brimstone (sulphur) on the shore of Whitstable... It will rise to a good commodity."*

The 'stranger' was probably Cornelius Stevenson, who was granted control over the copperas sites at Whitstable in 1565 but production did not start until around 1588, when Cornelius Stevenson's name first appears in parish records as giving money to the poor.

The erosion of the London clay by wave action washed out the copperas 'stones', as they were termed, to form part of the foreshore material. The nodules when broken open would show a radial structure with a brassy metallic colour, and hence were called 'gold stones' (occurrences of iron pyrites are often referred to as 'fool's gold'). Yet another name used was 'sulphur stones' because of the chemical nature of copperas: iron sulphide.

These nodules were collected and deposited in long beds or 'pannells', some as long as 116 feet by 15 feet wide, with shelving sides down to a depth of six feet, and being made impervious with packed clay.

When exposed to the elements, a weathering process took place resulting in oxidation, where a complex cycle of bacterial action took place.

This process resulted in the gradual leaking out of a dilute solution of hydrated ferrous sulphate ($FeSO_4$) and sulphuric acid (H_2SO_4). It was reckoned that it took up to four years for a bed to become fully 'ripe' or mature.

The liquid from the beds was conveyed down channels into several cisterns from which it was pumped, as required, into a huge lead boiler, usually some twelve feet square, positioned over a number of furnaces to produce the necessary high temperature.

This process needed an enormous quantity of coal; about 100lbs. of scrap iron was placed in the boiler at the beginning, with another 1,500lbs being added during the process, to help control the concentration of the sulphuric acid. A 'boiling' might continue for some 20 days.

When the 'liquor' was judged ready, it was passed along a lead channel into large lead tanks, or 'coolers', where it would remain for around 14 days. As it cooled, the crystals of ferrous sulphate would form by precipitation on the bottom and sides, and often on bundles of twigs which were hung down into the tank.

When it was considered that this process was complete, the 'cooler' was drained, the excess liquid returned to be reused, and the crystals shovelled onto a board surface to drain and dry.

Thus 'green vitriol', ferrous sulphate, was achieved. The crystals, also called copperas, were packed into barrels or casks for transporting.

It is still possible to find copperas along the surface of the shingle bank, the Street, at Tankerton.

Information from 'Copperas and the Castle' by Geoffrey Pike.

PEARSON AND STEAM

In 1773 King George III was on the throne and Captain James Cook became the first European explorer to cross the Antarctic Circle.

Parliament passed the Tea Act, designed to save the British East India Company by granting it a monopoly on the North American tea trade.

The Manor of Tankerton and the surrounding works were inherited by Elizabeth Radford, daughter of William and Elizabeth, of Thames Ditton, Surrey, from her uncle John Stiegler of Esher.

In 1775, the site of the present castle was occupied by a house that had been owned by Nicholas Sympson who built the copperas works. John Stiegler was a cooper and copperas merchant. In 1769 he purchased the 'Outlets' Works at a cost of £900.

Charles Pearson

The following year he acquired the Old Mascall Works for £576 13s 6d. The deed also indicates that he already owned land to the east which had belonged to Mary Godfrey.

Stiegler died in 1773 and his estate, with these copperas interests, was inherited by his niece Elizabeth Radford of Ludgate Hill, in the City of London. The comments in a later diary kept by her daughter Elizabeth suggest that she was a very shrewd, thrifty, and hard-working woman with no social pretensions.

Aged 27, Elizabeth did not attempt to rid herself of her industrial inheritance, but entered into an agreement with the 'Co-Partnership' for a £500 block of shares. In 1777, presumably finding this a profitable investment, she added the New Mascall Works to her holding for £1200.

In 1780 Elizabeth Radford married London businessman Charles Pearson and this union launched the last stage in the story of the Whitstable copperas industry.

Although Elizabeth Radford owned the rights to the copperas, the Lord of the Manor 1n 1790 was George Richard St. John Lord Viscount Bolingbroke.

He was married to lady Diana Spencer, daughter of the third Duke of Marlborough. She had three children – George, Charles and Elizabeth.

The artist Joshua Reynolds was a close family friend of the Bolingbrokes.

Charles Pearson of Ravensbourne House, Greenwich, was a member of the Glovers Company.

The trading interests of Pearson in London were complemented by the involvement in the copperas industry that provided fabric and leather dyes.

It is noted that a Whitstable copperas works owner paid for a massive system of sea defences to protect the site from rising water levels.

Pearson acquired the land at Tankerton and also the title 'Lord of the Manor'.

The Pearsons had four children; Elizabeth, Charles, Clara and Amelia. They stayed in the manor from July till the end of October.

The copperas industry however was in decline as workers found that there was more to be made in Native Oyster farming. Pearson began demolishing the copperas works and used the bricks to add an octagonal tower.

Little is known about its layout except that in 1798, as Elizabeth Pearson writes, "The hall chimney has been taken down and a staircase made in its place". Recent research by the author has shown that the house was around 14 feet x 35 feet.

The Pearsons lived in Ravensbourne House, Greenwich, but every summer they travelled by hoy or coach to Whitstable where they would have off-loaded on what is now known as 'The Street' – a spit of land about half a mile long stretching out into the Thames Estuary. At low tide one can walk along the exposed shingle and get another perspective of the town.

Pearson Goes To Court

'On Tuesday last a cause of considerable importance to those interested in manorial rights was tried at Maidstone before Lord Kenyon, wherein Charles Pearson, Esq., Lord of the Manor of Whitstable, was Plaintiff; and Mr Foord, a gentleman in the neighbourhood of Canterbury, of considerable property, Defendant.

The Defendant had enclosed a piece of waste upon Bostal Hill, adjoining his own land; to try his right to which the present action was brought; when, after hearing three witnesses, the right of the Plaintiff to all the waste land upon this extensive manor was clearly and fully established, by a verdict of the Jury, given under the direction of Lord Kenyon, who remarked in the course of the evidence that not only all waste lands, but deserted roads, and mines, should there be any under them, were the property of the Lord of the Manor.'

From Bell's Weekly Messenger (London, England), Sunday, August 2, 1801; Issue 276.

In 1810, George IV was on the throne and Charles Pearson Jnr married Eliza Justly-Hill Daughter of Lt-Col Justly-Hill of the Royal Artillery and Bengal Artillery. She died in 1850. They had eight children.

Charles Pearson Snr embarked on a new venture - 'The Canterbury and Whitstable Railway'. This was done in conjunction with George Stephenson and his cousin, Robert. Is it possible that they spent some time at the castle?

William IV succeeded his brother, George IV, at the age of 64 in 1830 and the New London Bridge was opened over the River Thames. Dickens published 'Oliver Twist', drawing attention to Britain's poor.

Charles Darwin returned from a five year voyage on HMS Beagle, researching natural history.

The Canterbury and Whitstable Railway opened on 3 May 1830, four months before the Liverpool and Manchester Railway which is often (incorrectly!) quoted as being the world's first railway. The Canterbury and Whitstable line was the first in the world to carry fare-paying passengers and issue season tickets. It also boasted the world's first railway tunnel and railway bridge!

Engineered by George and Robert Stephenson, the 5¾ mile line ran from Canterbury to Whitstable Harbour, pulled by three stationary winding engines, and 'Invicta'.

The Invicta was an 0-4-0 locomotive, built by the Stevenson company, but it only operated on a level section of track because she produced insufficient power (9hp).

Pearson died in 1828, two years before the railway opened. His son Charles Pearson Junior inherited the estate and carried on using the house as a summer residence.

The Tower became neglected and Charles Pearson Junior sold it to Wynn Ellis.

ART AND LOVER

Wynn Ellis was born in July 1790 at Oundle, Northamptonshire, the surviving son of Thomas Ellis of Flint, mid Wales – a coachman at the Talbot Inn – and Elizabeth Ordway of Barkway, Hertfordshire. *(There was an earlier son which sadly died just 17 months old.)*

In notes made by John Clifton, an Oundle carpenter who did a lot of work for Thomas Ellis at the Talbot, Ellis's marriage is mentioned:

> *March 14 1771 Mr T Ellis married today in London.*

He was educated at Oundle School whose origins lie in Sir William Laxton's endowment to the Worshipful Company of Grocers to re-establish a school in Oundle.

Wynn Ellis MP

Subsequently the lure of London beckoned and, in 1812, he became a haberdasher, hosier, and mercer at 16 Ludgate Street, City of London, where he gradually created the largest silk business in London, adding shop to shop as the property around him became vacant, and moving from retail into the wholesale business in 1830.

Ellis and his partner were involved in the earliest of the major UK cases in 1836 between Chas Macintosh & Co. as plaintiffs and Wynne Ellis as defendant. The plaintiff's case was that Everington and Ellis had infringed Charles Macintosh's patent of 1823 for the manufacture of 'double textured' cloth.

They won their case but opposition to an extension of the patent was so great that they decided to withdraw it and, at last, opted for the only protection left – to patent both the masticator and the spreading machinery.

Wynn Ellis MP

In 1831 Wynn decided to enter into politics but he withdrew his candidature as alderman for the ward of Castle Baynard to contest the parliamentary seat of Leicester. He was an advanced liberal and held the seat from May 4, 1831 to December 29, 1834, and again from March 22, 1839 to July 23, 1847.

He was an advocate for the total repeal of the Corn Laws, of free trade generally, of reform in bankruptcy, and of greater freedom in the law of partnership. In the committees of the House of Commons he applied considerable influence.

He was a Justice of the Peace both for Hertfordshire and Kent, and was nominated to serve as sheriff for the latter, but was excused on reflection of his having been a JP for Hertfordshire in 1851-2.

His political speeches can be found in Hansard via the Portcullis House website.

After his retirement in 1871 from his London business his firm assumed the title of John Howell & Co.

He became well known as the Liberal MP for Hertford, a magistrate and public figure. He was also a collector of fine arts.

He made the most significant impact and the greatest contribution towards shaping the castle building and grounds.

He married Mary Maria Smith, the ward of Charles Pearson.

Unfortunately Mary Maria was of a sickly disposition so it was with his mistress that Wynn Ellis sought a family.

Mary Maria Ellis, née Smith

Susan Lloyd was in service as a kitchen maid to Richard Edmond St Lawrence Boyle, Earl of Cornwall, and bore him a daughter, Susan Alinda, in 1825.

Susan's mother fell ill and was unable to bear him any more offspring.

It was about this time that Jane Graystone enters the scene and she gave birth to a son in 1835.

The only record of Jane is as follows, printed as it was received:

> GRAYSTONE, Arthur Conrad
> Matric. 1852,
> LL.B.1859, LL.M. 1862.
> 14 October 1852, p., Messrs Burnell and Atlay.
> Son of Jane Graystone.
> County Middlesex; born at St George, Hanover Square, 14 January 1835.
> Certificate from Edward John May, M.A.
> Parkinson Papers: There in a declaration made at the Mansion House, London, by Thomas Parker, of The Brook, Lamberhurst, Sussex, and 23 Spring Gardens, Westminster, stating that he is the guardian of A.C Graystone, son of Jane Graystone, formerly of Trellick Terrace, Pimlico, Middlesex, deceased. That A.C. Graystone was born 14 January 1835 and baptised in St George, Hanover Square, when the said Thomas Parker was present. The birth and baptism are not registered.

Susan Lloyd

As to Jane's demise, there is no record.

The connection between Ellis and Graystone is not clear, but at some time they obviously became closely acquainted as Arthur Graystone moved into the Towers and later inherited the estate.

Arthur Graystone studied divinity at Cambridge. He attended St John's as a pensioner (that is an ordinary fee-paying student) in 1852 to study the Law Tripos. He graduated in 1859 and, although he did not seem to excel academically, he gained a Third Class in his Civil Law papers for 1855-1856. After this, he was ordained and served in various parishes.

He married Emily Twiss, of Cambridge, in 1861. Emily survived him, dying in 1903.

Meanwhile, Wynn Ellis repaired the building, removed the ivy and laid foundations for a new West wing and Bell Tower furthest from the original tower – this was finished in 1840.

By 1842 he had built North Lodge, which stood where the front car park is, and South Lodge which stood behind the present toilet block.

The estate, including fields, cottages, gravel pits and beach extended from Bennells Avenue to Oxford Street at the other end of Whitstable. In the grounds, which extended down to the shore, there were stables, summerhouses, an ice house, vegetable and flower gardens as well as tennis courts and other sports facilities.

He bought several more properties for Susan Lloyd Snr in Whitstable.

Susan didn't always stay at Tankerton, although she left a housekeeper there. In 1850, Ellis added a conservatory to the Tower. Susan died in 1869 – the same year as the Great Fire of Whitstable.

Wynn Ellis was responsible for the castellation of the Manor House and he stayed at Tankerton Tower each summer and led a full social life.

He was often seen riding out on 'The Street', (a promontory reaching out into the sea) on a goat cart.

His wife Mary Maria died in 1892 childless; her remains were brought to Whitstable from Hatfield.

Wynn Ellis was a sponsor of the local Tankerton Regatta that is now an annual event. He built almshouses, on the site of the Pearson Hotel at the bottom of Tower Hill, in memory of his wife.

Wynn Ellis died in London in November 1875 and his body was brought to Whitstable by special train and met by notable people in the area including the Vicar, the Rev H Maugham – the Uncle of Somerset Maugham, the playwright and novelist.

The funeral cortege was ornate; all the shops closed and his son, the Rev Arthur Graystone, helped to conduct the service. Wynn Ellis was then buried in the imposing mausoleum *(see below)* built on land he had given to All Saints Church. This can still be seen on the south-west side of the churchyard.

The Wynn Ellis Mausoleum in All Saints' Churchyard, Whitstable
Over the door is the inscription 'IANVA VITAE' meaning 'Gate of Life', and the date MDCCCLXXV (1875)

His Legacy was bequeathed to Miss Susan Alinda Lloyd, his daughter from his first mistress, and she became the Lady of the Manor.

Retaining her mother's name, Miss Lloyd spent each summer at Tankerton. She was of a retiring nature and suffered from ill-health. On the death of her mother she had the old coach house converted into the rather charming Albion Cottage for a more congenial home. Today this lies just outside the gatehouse. Miss Lloyd supported local good causes and allowed charity events to take place in the grounds of the Tower.

She died in 1884 and was buried alongside her mother in Kensal Green cemetery.

The Ellis estate passed to the Rev Graystone, who lived in Lancaster Gate, London. It was he who arranged the disposal of the art collection to The National Gallery, London.

He left two sons and the estate then passed to the elder, Sydney Wynn Graystone. He was also a student at Downing College, at Cambridge University, and is listed in 'Venn'.

> *Venn, J. A., comp. Alumni Cantabrigienses, Vol. 3. London: Cambridge University Press, 1940. Shows Graystone, Sydney Wynn. Adm. at CLARE, Jan. 27, 1881. S. and h. of Arthur Conrad (1852), clerk. B. 1862. School, Tonbridge.] Matric. Lent, 1881. Migrated to Downing, Oct. 14, 1882; B.A. 1885. Adm. at the Inner Temple,*
> *Oct. 31, 1884, age 22, as Sidney Wynn Graystone. of Cheveley Park, Cambs.*
> *High Sheriff of Cambs. and Hunts., 1912. Lord of the manor of Tankerton, Kent.*
> *Died Feb. 8, 1924. Benefactor to Downing. (Tonbridge Sch. Reg. (Sydney))*

(Venn wrote a biographical list of all known Students, Graduates and Holders of Office at the University of Cambridge, from the earliest times to 1900.)

Arthur Graystone became the new Lord of the Manor. Having inherited the bulk of his father's fortune, he was said to have been the wealthiest Church of England cleric ever, leaving a fortune of £4 million upon his death.

He continued to use Tankerton Tower in summer and played a part in the local community, supporting charities and events, and he founded the Masonic Lodge on Cromwell Road Whitstable. In 1879, it is recorded that Rev Arthur Graystone was charged with indecent assault. However, he was acquitted and, on his death at the age of 50, in 1886, the Whitstable Times commented that "His desire was to do good and, above all, his heart was for the welfare of Whitstable."

The elder of Rev Graystone's sons, Sydney Wynn Graystone, inherited the estate at the age of 24. He also graduated from St Johns, Cambridge. He was a yachtsman and had become a member of the cricket club and, in 1887, following the meeting of the Court Baron, he gave a grand dinner at the Bear and Key, in Whitstable, to celebrate the Jubilee Year.

When local gentlemen met to consider their candidate for the new County Council, Sydney Graystone was proposed and duly elected.

This same time, in 1887, the Trustees of Tankerton Tower and the lands of the estate sold the estate to a London barrister, Charles Newton-Robinson, although Sydney continued to act as Lord of the Manor.

In 1890 he moved to Devon and the estate was sold on his behalf for £22,000 and rented out for several years to Charles Edmund Newton Robinson.

THE PEN IS MIGHTIER THAN THE SWORD

Born 16th October 1853 in Kensington London, Charles Edmund Newton Robinson was the eldest son of Sir John Charles Robinson CB., of Newton Manor, Swanage. His mother was Marian Elizabeth Newton, of Norwich, from whom he took the name 'Newton'.

Charles Edmond was educated at Westminster School London and at Trinity College, Cambridge and was called to the Bar in 1879, aged 22.

He married Jane Anna, second daughter of Robert Smirke, an English architect, and one of the leaders of Greek revival architecture. Smirke designed the facade of the British Museum.

Charles Edmund Newton Robinson

At Westminster, he was 'Head of the Water' for two years running. At Cambridge he went in for running and hurdle jumping. He crossed the North Sea in a ten-ton yacht in 1874 and explored the Dutch Canals, and he gaily describes this trip in 'The Cruise of the Widgeon'.

He developed a passion for yacht-racing which lasted throughout his life. He built and sailed a long series of small racing yachts through quite thirty seasons of the Solent and South Coast Club Regattas. These lovely and workman-like little craft were often partly designed, steered and captained, by him; he won abundant laurels. In one season the yacht 'Corolla' took thirty-nine prizes out of fifty-one starts in the Solent Matches.

Jane Anna Robinson, née Smirke

He was a member of the Council of the Yacht Racing Association to his death, and took an eager and competent share in the discussion of technicalities of design and sailing regulations. However, he was best known as a fencer and he studied the épée in Paris under Anthime Spinnewyn.

In 1900 he invited his fencing master to visit London with some pupils to demonstrate the art of the épée to British fencers.

He was not only an expert swordsman in England and on the Continent but he interested himself warmly in the revival of swordsmanship in England. His favourite weapon was the épée de combat or duelling sword, and he persuaded a group of enthusiasts to establish the Épée Club of London in 1900.

Thirteen competitors took part in the first open épée tournament on 5 May 1900 and Newton-Robinson came second to the Frenchman Willy Sulzbacher, receiving a handsome silver medal for being the highest placed Englishman.

On 1 June of that year in Paris he became the first British fencer to take part in an Olympic Games, going out in the first round of the épée tournament.

Charles was captain of the British épée team that fenced in the Coupe International in Paris in 1904.

Two years later, at the age of 52, he was the oldest member of the British team that held France to a draw in the final of the Interim Olympics in Athens.

His achievements, however, were not recognised by the International Olympics Committee (IOC).

Several years after his death, his widow Jane gave the medals he had won at various competitions to the son of a friend, because the boy collected coins and she thought he might like them.

In 2004 that man, Peter Riddle, offered them to the National Fencing Museum (11 medals including the bronze medal he won in Athens in 1906).

At the 1908 London Olympic Games he received a silver-gilt commemorative medal for helping to organise those Games.

They are now in the National Fencing Museum.

The Art he loved most was poetry, and this was how he wished to be remembered.

In the free moments left him by a busy life he could always be found with pen in hand, and he laboured incessantly at the craftsmanship of poetry.

His first published volume of verse was 'The Golden Hind', a narrative poem to which various ballads and lyrics were added. 'Tintinnabula' (1) followed in 1890, 'The Viol of Love' (2) in 1895, and 'Ver Lyrae' (3) in 1896. This last is a volume of his collected poems with some later pieces added. 1,2,3, are still available.

'Moods and Metres' was contemplated before the long fatal illness began; extreme bodily weakness seemed to focus his mind in his last months on what most profoundly moved him, and even rendered it to his own feeling more lucid and ready. He did not live to see his works published, but his signature to the contract for its publication was the last word he ever wrote.

In 'Moods and Metres', New Lyric Poems, published in the Westminster Times of 1910, we find this poem – was it written for the towers?

AN OLD MANOR HOUSE

Dear home of mine! The morning sun
Lights yet thy rugged stones;
Though thrice a hundred years at rest
Have lain thy builder's bones:
Fathers and mothers, boys and girls
Now generations nine,
Thy fore-possessors' frames are dust;
The sun still cheereth thine.

Though thrice thine elms have grown and died,
Elms wave around thee still;
Where rooks of ancient pedigree
Yet quarrel, bill to bill:
And in this autumn of the year
And autumn of thy days,
The old grey church on Sundays yet
Peals out for thee God's praise.

A sanctuary thy garden is,
Stone walled and hedged with yew:
About, around, the oft-turned ground
Still beareth rose and rue:
And still the orchard reddeneth,
The fig, the vine, the quince
Still ripen full their honeyed fruit
As generations since.

The golden wagtail on the lawn
Trips fearless at his will:
Red robin hoppeth on and off
Thy hospitable sill:
The timid martin houses him
Below thy sheltering eaves,
While cheery Rover keeps his watch
As much for cats, as thieves.

And over all the master's eye
Roams lovingly and long:
The wreck of winters he repairs
To keep thee sound and strong.
He too hath weathered many storms
Unshaken, undismayed,
Ere children of his children came
To play, where once he played.

And she, the mistress of his house
And mistress of his heart,
At open door and open board
Still acts her gracious part,
As when they first together faced
A world they hardly knew,
In all the fearless pride of youth,
Each to the other true.

Dear house! Farewell
but not for long,
Though I go seeking gain,
And strive and fight with all my might
In cities, on the main:
In desert lands, 'mid whirling sands
Or furious mountain-snows;
Someday, like Robin, I'll return,
Dear home! to thy repose.

Charles Newton-Robinson 1910

Charles Newton-Robinson will be remembered by those who knew him not only by his gifts and accomplishments, but also as a man of amiable character, and one capable of deep and constant affection. He was an idealist through all his practical activities.

Poetry to him was the atmosphere of life, and its true spiritual reality. The tender halo of feeling through which he had his vision of life clings delicately around his poems.

The son of one of the greatest authorities and collectors of the Victorian Period, whose pioneer work enhances the South Kensington Museum to an extent only realised by those familiar with the provenance of many of its finest acquisitions.

Charles inherited the wide range of his father's taste with much of his self-reliance and independence of contemporary fashions and expertise.

His father collected eagerly and diversified in various directions, and formed an important Collection of Drawings by the Old Masters and of ancient engraved Gems and Cameos.

Of these last he made a special study, the fruits of which appeared in the Catalogue Raisonne in the Greek Exhibition in the Burlington Fine Arts Club in 1903.

He had also in preparation a book on the subject, but unfortunately this was unfinished.

He wrote from time to time many critical papers for both French and English Art periodicals.

But the son was less specialised than the father into the pursuit of Art, he scattered his energies over many activities in business, politics, and sport.

The more professional side of his life was occupied with Land Development: The town of Lee-on-the-Solent, often referred to as Lee-on-Solent, is a coastal town in Hampshire, England, about five miles west of Portsmouth. It is located on the coast of the Solent and forms part of the borough of Gosport.

It is primarily a residential area, but is well known as home to the Royal Naval Air Station HMS Daedalus and this town owes its existence largely to his efforts, as does Tankerton, in Kent.

It was the Land Taxes of the Budget of 1909-10 that roused him to take an active part in politics and inspired him to organise the foundation of the 'Land Union' to resist ill-considered interference with the interests of owners of land. As usual he threw himself heart and soul into this agitation, and wrote the clever parody, 'Alice in Plunderland' (under a pseudonym) as well as the pamphlet called 'The Blight of the Land Taxes', and many other ephemeral articles.

In July 1890, he formed The Tankerton Estate Company.

This Company was set-up with capital almost all pledged by Newton-Robinson, along with another barrister and businessman Edward Bond and the distinguished architect Basil Champneys who designed more notable buildings including Newnham College, Cambridge; Manchester's John Rylands Library; Mansfield College, Oxford; and Oriel College, Oxford's Rhodes Building.

In August the Company purchased from Newton-Robinson (for £23,600) the entire seaward side of the estate bounded on the south and west by the railway lines. This therefore included the Tower in which he had been living although he retained the other farmland and the manorial title.

As the Company's brochure stated, the plan was 'the complete development of this magnificent property as a new Watering Place of the first class ... now for the first time Tankerton has been opened up to the public, there seems a high probability that its beauty and advantages will be appreciated and its success assured.'

The outline plan published showed wide boulevards linked with a grid pattern of residential roads, an open 'Kingsdown Park', and sites for rows of shops and a number of hotels. They envisaged a miniature Eastbourne on the north Kent coast.

In June 1891, the first of a long series of land auctions was launched in an extravagant manner.

To raise much needed capital the Company planned to sell the house, with its extensive grounds down to the cliffs and the beach, for £10,000. It was now more grandly called the 'Towers'.

The road known as Tower Road that runs between the cliff and the Castle was part of Robinson's plan.

The 1890s were years of economic depression, and no buyers were to be found. It was then decided to let the property for £250 per year.

THE PLAYWRIGHT

The only tenant was the playwright Sir Arthur Wing Pinero, the celebrated dramatist who had heard of the property from other stage personalities who often visited Whitstable.

Sir Arthur Wing Pinero was an English actor and later an important dramatist and stage director.

Born May 24, 1855, in London – died November 23, 1934, London, a leading playwright of the late Victorian and Edwardian eras in England, he made an important contribution toward creating a self-respecting theatre by helping to found a 'social' drama that drew a fashionable audience. It is his farces – literate, superbly constructed, with a precise, clockwork inevitability of plot and a brilliant use of coincidence – that have proved to be of lasting value.

Sir Arthur Wing Pinero

Born into an English family descended from Portuguese Jews, Pinero abandoned legal studies at age 19 to become an actor; and, though still a young man, he played older characters.

Pinero was born in London, the son of a Sephardic Jewish solicitor, John Daniel Pinero. He studied law at Birkbeck Literary and Scientific Institution before going on the stage.

It is said his appearance was a little surprising and his eyebrows featured prominently. It was said "They were the skins of some small mammal just not large enough to be used as mats."

In 1889 he married Myra Emily Holme, daughter of Beaufoy Amoore and widow of Captain John Angus L Hamilton. She died in 1919.

He is best known for his comedies: The Magistrate (1885); Dandy Dick (1887); The Cabinet Minister (1890); The Notorious Mrs Ebbsmith (1895); Trelawny of the 'Wells' (1898); and The Gay Lord Quex (1899).

It seems the Pineros had no lasting impact on the castle. Mrs Pinero, however, is credited with putting the first horse trough outside the Toll House at the foot of Borstal Hill by the junction with Joy Lane.

They lived at the towers for only six months, from June to December 1893.

Myra Emily Pinero, née Holme

THE MYSTERY OWNER

Thomas Edward Adams was born in the district of St Thomas, Exeter, Devon, in the January – March quarter of 1859.

He married Sarah Gwynfred Stevens at Richmond, Surrey in 1882 and their daughter, Gwynfred Constance, was born in Staines in the following year.

When Thomas Adams bought the house in 1897 from the Tankerton Estate company which had acquired the property after Wynn Ellis's death, the new gatehouse was built, and the building was renamed 'The Towers'.

Thomas can be found in the 1861 Census for South Molton, a district of Exeter.

According to the census for 1891 he was not living at Tankerton Towers. There appears to be a Thomas John Taylor and his wife Jane. He was a Gardener Servant and she is shown as the Caretaker.

Thomas appears in the 1901 Census for Whitstable as "living on own means".

He died in the spring of 1902, aged 42.

After his death his wife married Mr Neal Argent, and they lived in the castle for a further 20 years.

> *Thomas Edward Adams is the only occupant of the castle I have had difficulty finding anything about at this time. Research at the West Country Library turned up no real insight into his life.*
>
> *It is recorded, however, that he built the gatehouse at the bottom of Castle Hill; also that he built a large room to the north of the Pearson tower. More research is needed. Ed.*

THE END OF AN ERA

The Castle passed into the hands of Mr Albert Mallandain, who was to become the last occupant of The Towers, in 1921.

The Mallandain family were originally from the Normandy, Picardy and Brittany regions of France and they were among thousands of French Protestants, or Huguenots, who fled to England to escape religious persecution. The first migrants settled in London's East End, primarily in the Tower Hamlets of Stepney, Shoreditch, Bethnal Green and Spitalfields area of London. Here, they became part of the French refugee community of master silk weavers.

The Mallandain name appears first in Canterbury at the time of the revocation of the Edict of Nantes in 1685.

Albert was born on 12 July 1866 in Walworth, Surrey, now part of southeast London.

He appears in the 1881 census, living with his family at 65 Leipsic Road in Camberwell and working as a Draughtsman's Assistant. He also appears in the 1892 Post Office Directory as a Draughtsman at 1 & 2 Poultry, EC. In the 1895 Directory, his business address was recorded as 51 Cheapside.

He married Florence Welton on 16 July 1896 at Christ Church in Lambeth. His occupation was now listed as Lithographer and he lived at The Vicarage on Camberwell Road. Florence was born in Deptford in 1872, the daughter of Charles Welton, a gentleman. She lived at Grove Park, Camberwell at the time of her marriage.

Albert and Florence did not have any children.

The Mallandains had a Rolls Royce, but Albert often walked to the station each morning, leaving by the exit in The Tower, instead of the main entrance down to the gateway.

He and his wife lived at The Towers from June until September and he maintained the life of a country gentleman in grand style. They enjoyed entertaining: *"there were frequent weekend house parties and their annual Garden Party was the social event of the Whitstable calendar."*

They also took an active role in assisting the residents of the local almshouses by employing a nurse to care for them, and organizing an annual coach trip. Florence died in Westminster in 1951 and Albert died at Copsem Manor, Surrey, on 24 November 1956.

Albert left an estate valued at £205,788; when his will was signed in August 1955, his sister Rose Emma was his only surviving sibling. He left his house at 32 Wyatt Park Road in Streatham to her but she died three months before him.

She was living in the house as early as 1928, up to her death in August 1956.

There were two significant additions to the building during these later years: At the south end, a large conservatory was built providing a very sunny space to the generally rather gloomy interior. In the Mallandains' time there was a central marble statue with a fountain surrounded by a collection of choice tropical plants. The date of this feature is uncertain; probably it was one of the improvements made by Mr Adams. At the north end of the house, Mr Mallandain added a large two storey block, faithfully copying the materials and castellated style of the existing fabric.

The ground floor contained the billiard room, an essential feature for a country house of the time. It was elaborately panelled, with an ornate fireplace and furnished with tapestry-covered chairs. Here guests would usually gather for coffee after dinner.

Kate Anderson

Kate Anderson joined the staff at the Castle as a parlour maid in 1924 where she looked after three other female staff. She described life at the elegantly furnished home as hard work, with one half-day off per week and pay of £2 per month plus board and lodging.

> *"There were many stairs to run up and down – the Master bedroom was on the top of The Tower, where the Mallandains had their breakfast.*
>
> *A grandfather clock stood in the hallway and the drawing room had a log fire showing up the tapestries."*

But Kate had happy memories of her time there and the entertaining of weekend guests. She was one of four household staff and was later to marry the gardener, Harry Anderson, who worked in the grounds.

Transcript of News Item – 1977

"Upstairs, Downstairs" was the hit TV drama of the early 1970s, which so many people enjoyed, about the lives of domestic servants in the house of a well-to-do family, and of the master and mistress of the house.

This series, according to Mrs Kate Anderson of Whitstable, is a perfectly accurately portrayal: Kate spent five years as a housemaid at the Castle when it was owned by Mr and Mrs Albert Mallandain, although Kate said they lived there only during the summer months from June to September. They kept their servants on their toes with numerous guests, dinner parties, garden parties and all kinds of social events.

"It was a hard life," Kate recalled, "we had to work hard, but I enjoyed it." She was 19 when she came to the Towers, (in 1924) young by today's standards, but at that time a girl of 19 had several years work experience behind her, for she had often left school before her 14th birthday.

Working as a housemaid was poorly paid, with long hours and little free time.

Kate's day started at around 5:30 each morning. She would make morning tea and clean the stairs and hall before the master and mistress of the house were up.

She helped the parlour maid serve at table, made the beds, cleaned the rooms, and cleaned the visitors' shoes which they left outside their doors.

There were few labour-saving devices to clean such a large place, and Kate remembers particularly cleaning the large amount of wood surfaces in the house. "We used to wash the wood-work with vinegar and warm water – we must have used gallons of vinegar!" she said.

Her three fellow workers in the house were her cousin Muriel Alexander, a kitchen maid; parlour maid Kate Coomber (now Mrs Neame) and cook/housekeeper Mrs Warnerhen.

They would have been 'watched', as they went about their duties, by the Shakespearean characters looking down from the frieze around the Mallandain's bedroom. *(see next page)*

Kate died in 1983 and is buried in All Saints churchyard.

It had always been assumed Kate Anderson was married to Paddy Walker but she is interred as Kate Anderson along with her husband Harry.

Philip Nutten, whose mother remembered Paddy Walker, says:

> *"My mum confirmed that Paddy Walker was the gardener there around the mid to late 50's, she couldn't remember who he married but she was positive her maiden name wasn't Anderson. Primarily he looked after the grounds but also worked on other flower beds around the town.*

From my own memory, Paddy Walker had left this job and was employed on the Council's general labour force by 1964 and Charles Spearing was the senior (working) gardener in the Castle greenhouses until a new 'Parks and Gardens Manager' David Harrison was appointed over him."

THE MALLANDAIN FRIEZE
(see previous page)

Abbess
'Comedy of Errors'

Launce
'Two Gentlemen of Verona'

The Clown

The King

Prospero
'The Tempest'

Malcolm
'Macbeth'

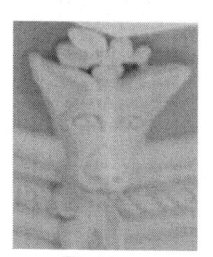

Bottom
'Midsummer Night's Dream'

Julius Caesar

THE BUILDING OF THE CASTLE

This section will look at the development of the castle from Elizabeth Radford's house to the building we have today. Records of the changes are thin at best.

The footprint of the original house is, in the main, lost in the up-grading of the property over the years. The original building as described in 'Pearson and Steam' looks to have been 14 feet by 35 feet.

The house is set in the Tankerton slopes facing west.

It was originally a two-story construction with the main front door facing the gardens. There was a drainage ditch around three sides to prevent the ground water from the higher garden entering the house.

Part of this can still be seen to the left of the main entrance.

The first major work to the property was undertaken by Charles Pearson when he built the tower to the northeast corner using the flint and bricks from the disused copperas works.

Was this an early form of recycling?

He also added the staircase just inside the main door by removing a fireplace in 1798.

With growing children he decided to add to the existing tower a new block matching the existing style with battlement roofline.

Shortly after Elizabeth Pearson senior's death in 1817, he handed over the running of the estate to their son, Charles Pearson Jnr.

By now, the young Charles had a growing family so he decided to enlarge the house from the Gothic style of his father into a Tudor style. An etching of 1828 shows an outline of a low single storey structure on the west elevation of the house (now the castle dining room and kitchen.)

With the aid of Mr Inman, of Harbledown, work commenced on 10th August 1820 with the first brick being laid of a modest manor house.

When finished, Charles' sister Elizabeth wrote:

> "The house was big enough for the six members of the family, their servants and overnight visitors."

The Swalecliffe Brickworks were possibly a provider of bricks, for the remodelling, being the local producer for Victorian Whitstable.

Charles Pearson Senior's works of 1790 were rebuilt by his son, though the earlier Gothic sash windows and internal plasterwork of the lower part of the Tower, along with the Victorian solid wooden panel shutters to the windows in the Pearson Tower, remain.

Wynn Ellis bought the property in 1833 and, over time, became the largest landowner in Whitstable. His properties stretched from the top of Oxford Street in the west to Bennells Avenue in the east and from the Thanet Way in the south to the sea in the north.

He set his mind to the problems he had taken on. Charles Pearson Junior's son, Charles Hill Pearson, born in 1811, acted as overseer.

The house at this time consisted of the main East Block at basement, ground and first floor.

A small South Block, projecting from the South West corner of the East Block joined the original house to the west wing.

The whole South Block appears to have been demolished a few years later by Wynn Ellis to make way for his big square Tower and circular Stair and Bell Towers. There are signs of a blocked-up window in the gents' toilets. This can also be seen in the etching of 1828.

Tankerton Tower remained very much the seaside villa it had developed into under the ownership of the Pearsons.

Wynn Ellis started to enlarge the Tower and re-organised and altered the interior of the building.

Along the west side, to open the view over the sea towards

Faversham and Sheppey, he built a long, two-floor range of reception rooms and bedrooms, placing the kitchen and its associated service spaces at the north end of the ground floor. The first floor room, now called the Robinson Room, was possibly a children's bedroom with the nanny's room being where the ladies toilet is now.

At the south end of the building Wynn Ellis added a Bell Tower and Clock Room. The new work was constructed of brick, faced entirely in Kent rag stone with French Caen stone surrounding the doors, windows and corners of the building. It was also used on the battlements.

With the addition of a series of square and round towers along with turrets and battlements, plus late mediaeval style windows and flat hood moulds, the castle effect was complete.

He also fitted out the interior with joinery and plaster in a mixture of Tudor and Elizabethan style, some of which can be seen at the south end of the first floor, in both sets of main stairs and in the second floor of the east block known as the Miles Room.

When the work on the Tower was finished, in the late 1840s, he had transformed the building into a small country house of a sort typically occupied by powerful and newly rich merchants who had prospered in the economic boom of the post-Napoleonic decades.

By the end of Wynn Ellis's developments he had extended the footprint of the house to approximately 31 feet x 61 feet.

It could be said that this was true Victorian eccentricity.

Wynn Ellis then turned his attention to landscaping the grounds, providing conservatories, hothouses and greenhouses, assisting local public building projects and attending to matters of estate management. Through the 1850's and 1860's he used Tankerton Tower increasingly, particularly in the summer, but apparently undertook no further alterations or improvements to the Castle.

The next phase of building took place in the late 1890 – early

1900s with the building of the north wing or Mallandain Room.

Queen Victoria was on the throne and it was an age of Empire building. It was also a time of tremendous change in the lives of British people.

In 1837 most people lived in villages and worked on the land; by 1901, most lived in towns and worked in offices and factories.

The Mallandains spent most of the time in London but, despite his age of 69 or 70, they still came to the Castle. His paper business was based in the City, at King's House, King Street, Cheapside, this was an address of commercial status, suggesting he remained prosperous.

They owned the Towers for 15 years, enlarging and altering it with the help of a local architect named Oswald Cane Wylson.

They used the building mainly for entertaining between June and September or at weekends.

Taking seriously their responsibilities towards the 'estate' they invested large amounts of money in the property and on the building fabric, both internally and externally.

Wylson was commissioned to design and build the two-floored, 'Gothic' style extension on the north end of the Castle. Its main function was to house a new Billiard Room, which were very popular in early Edwardian times.

On the first floor he provided servant bedrooms with access to the kitchen via service stairs.

Wylson also undertook major repairs to the building, both externally and internally.

He rendered over the decaying Caen stone dressings of Wynn Ellis's building, and replaced all the copings on the earlier battlements in Portland stone, to match the new extension.

At the south end, new lobbies and WC's were provided at both floor levels, between the stairs and Bell Tower: the first floor actually sits on top of what had been the Pearsons' South Porch.

Wylson re-organised and extensively re-finished in a reproduction Tudor/Elizabethan style.

Polished oak panelling was introduced throughout the ground floor, and the present oak stairs and landings were inserted. Plaster improvements were added to the ceiling of the Main Stair space showing the Tudor Rose of England, the portcullis of Westminster (recognising Wynn Ellis as MP) and the Fleur-de-Lis – Mallandains own sign as a Huguenot. Around the frieze of the vaulted ceiling, in the upper floor of the Pearson' Tower are plaster casts of Shakespearean characters.

The Graystone Room was reorganised and given its present Tudor style, oak wall alcoves. The fire was moved at some time from the west wall to the east and the framed tapestries, recently discovered in one of the Castle stores and restored, now hang in the Graystone Room.

The Wynn Ellis's interiors at the southern end of the lower ground floor were remodelled.

A number of walls were removed creating the present, rather irregularly shaped, Wynn Ellis Room (now part on the castle dining rooms) which he lined in panelling.

A large leaded-light window was inserted in the south wall to provide more daylight for the main stair.

And here the story ends for some unknown reason; the Mallandains never returned to the Castle after the summer of 1932 when they retired to Copsem Manor at Oxshott in Surrey.

It was the time of the Great Depression. They moved from their London and Whitstable homes to live quietly in Surrey. Albert died, aged 91, in 1956.

So ends the times of occupation of The Castle by the Sea as a home.

A NEW BEGINNING

In 1935 the building was bought by the Whitstable Urban District Council. The name was changed to 'Whitstable Castle' and it was to be used as local government offices – the billiard room was transformed into the council chamber.

The grounds were opened as a public park in the same year to mark the Royal Silver Jubilee and concerts and dances were held on the site of the tennis courts.

The Kitchen garden area was laid out as a bowling green and the tennis courts below the west front were converted for outdoor dancing. The grounds became a popular social centre.

After the war, the tennis courts were converted into a large entertainments area with a small covered stage. Here at the 'Pleasure Ground' bands played, and the floor could be laid for dancing. It remained a popular feature until the early 1950s when, with the advent of TV, this kind of entertainment waned. Today, this area forms the rose garden.

In 1948, an area of overgrown land across the road from the Castle, once, of course, within the original grounds, was laid out as Tea Gardens and Putting Green. This remains a popular venue in summer, though few who relax there over a cup of tea will realise that this was the site of a Copperas Works.

The North Lodge, which incorporated the last surviving building of the copperas works, was pulled down in 1960 to make way for a car park.

After the local government re-organisation in 1972 (when the council was established in Canterbury) the Castle remained empty until 1975 when, at the prompting of The Whitstable Society, the 'Castle Centre Association' was created with the aim of using The Castle for the benefit of the people of Whitstable.

A new Trust, 'The Whitstable Castle Trust', was formed in 2008 to take over the running of the Castle and Gardens.

The surrounding public park received a Heritage Lottery Fund and Big Lottery Fund grant award of £2,063,000 in June 2008.

This money, together with a contribution of £494,218 plus staff time and expertise from Canterbury City Council, enabled the Castle building and park to be made accessible and welcoming to visitors.

Today the building and gardens are used by many local people for a wide range of activities.

Each year the gardens are used by the local community for a series of charitable fund-raising events.

THE GARDENS

In the 1860s the gardens were considerably extended and landscaped.

It is possible that when garrya elliptica (silk tassel bush) was first introduced into Britain a specimen was planted in the Tower grounds.

In the gardens there are a large variety of unique plants which have been grown here since the gardens were first laid out in the 1780's. Some plants came from trips abroad by the owners of the house; visitors will see mature oak trees lining the Gate House drive, the Rose Garden is planted with roses and other climbers, all with beautiful scents filling the air as you wander under the grand pergola, listening to the restored central fountain.

The gardens have undergone a stunning transformation over an eighteen month period of restoration and redesign, supported by the National Lottery's 'Parks for People Fund' and Canterbury City Council.

On the lower terrace you will find borders filled with many varieties of plants. Seating is provided throughout to allow you to rest and take in the stunning views and fresh sea air. Just a short walk from the main Castle is the Castle Tea Gardens, with lush herbaceous borders and terraced lawns, once again with stunning views out to sea across the Thames Estuary to the Isle of Sheppey and beyond to the Essex coastline.

The current gardener, Dan Pretlove, came to the Castle from the Chelsea Physic Garden (London's oldest botanic garden) and is available to give guided tours (booking advised).

Thanks to Dan and a very able team of volunteers, the gardens are the wonderful sight they are today.

The gardens attract a variety of birds with nests being built in the trees and ivy borders. There are wood piles and old rotting tree stumps which attract beetles and other insects in large numbers.

We also plant a wide variety of high nectar yielding plants to attract other insects into the gardens; in 2009 the tea gardens became the home to hundreds of painted lady butterflies, blown in on the warm southerly winds from Europe.

Green Flag Award 2012

Whitstable Castle Gardens have become one of the most popular destinations locally since the restoration project was completed in September 2010. Extensive ground works have been undertaken to achieve this unique setting for the whole family and all abilities to enjoy every day of the year. No matter what the season there is always something different for one to see and enjoy in the gardens. Along with the hard landscaping there is also the addition of the new adventure play area containing a pirate ship, swing and roundabout.

The Castle Gardens have hosted many community events since re-opening, including the return of the Whitstable and Herne Bay Lions Club May Day Fair. Treasure hunts have been very popular and a Scarecrow Festival held in October 2011 attracted 30 entries and over 200 families taking part with a trail around the gardens. The Easter egg hunt proves to be a big hit with the younger children, with over 150 children with their families participating in 2012. Running alongside this were the craft workshops in the new Castle Studio, a wooden building erected in 2011 with help from funding given by the former Castle Centre Association.

During the summer, Whitstable Brass hold free open air concerts on the top terrace. The Tango proved very popular in July last year with a temporary dance floor installed in the Rose Garden. Also, a Pirate Treasure Hunt (as part of the Oyster Festival) brought families, not only from Whitstable and the district but from London and beyond.

Whitstable Castle Gardens have been recognised locally by winning the 2011 Best Public Open Space award and the coveted Green Flag award in 2012.

The Castle won several 'Whitstable In Bloom' accolades including winning a Bronze in 2010 for the Tea Garden, and silver in 2011 and 2012 for the Tea Gardens and Main Gardens.

The gardens attract a wide variety of wildlife including birds, insects, mammals, foxes, etc. Bats have returned to the Castle gardens and can be seen searching for food at dusk.

Stag beetles have always been a resident here and new habitats have been built to help with the protection of them. There was a pair of nesting blue tits in an unusual home – the column for the main car park CCTV camera! The pair could be seen busy returning to the nest with new nesting material and then with insects for the young.

Whitstable Art Society displayed their pictures in the Castle gardens in 2012, and several other local groups held a variety of events including sponsored walks to raise money for the Royal British Legion. The Alzheimer's Society will be returning for their Memory Walk in September, this year, after the success of last year's event which was officially started by Janet Street-Porter and the Lord Mayor of Canterbury.

The Castle Garden can also boast to having the biggest living Christmas tree in Kent. Adorned with some 500 LED energy efficient lights, the tree is lit in late November and stays on throughout December. Funding for the lights was promoted through local schools with a colouring competition. The scheme was completed in November 2010 and has become a focal point of celebrations for the community. The Castle hosts its own Christmas Fair in November along with other events throughout the festive season, including the open air Christmas market in December.

The Castle provides a unique and special venue for weddings, private parties, local classes, corporate and community events.

Group and School visits are welcomed and can be booked via the Castle office.

Whitstable Urban District Council

In 1936 the Whitstable Urban District Council took over the building and turned it into offices and I am grateful to Mr and Mrs Philip Nutten, who worked for the Council, for their information regarding the use of the rooms at that time.

The entrance for the public was via the lower door beside the bell tower.

The Chairman entered via the main castle door.

On the ground floor

The Orangery was the Planning office.

The room where the counter is was the typing pool.

The area where the fireplace is was the engineer's office.

The Kitchen was the office of the Chief Administration Officer.

The under croft housed the headquarters of the Civil Defence.

On the entrance floor

The Pearson Room was a reception area, and the Mallandain Room was the council chamber.

On the first floor

The Graystone and Robinson Rooms were the Town Clerks' offices.

The Miles Room was the office of the Leader of the Council.

The North and South Rooms

These rooms were for the Secretariat.

Tankerton Towers was, as I hope you have seen, first and foremost a family home.

The towers were built on the back of hard work and investment from copperas to haberdashery to paper.

Whitstable Castle is part of the story of the development of the town and the cloth-dying industry.

MEMORIES

Local residents recall their memories of the castle...

Mrs Reed told me:

> "In 1937 it was a meeting place. The castle was always an attraction, more so in the spring and summer. It was a romantic place then with outside dancing, fairy lights and a local band – Norman Perkins. The castle had lots of little walk-ways that sometimes led to small thatched huts to sit in. There were lots of trees and flowers. The other side of the road, where the tea garden is now, was a ruin. We used to imagine it was haunted. No doubt the improvements will bring money in but, for me, the romance of the place has gone."

The 'Ruins' Mrs Reed refers to were the remains of the old works, now the Tea Garden.

Marie Hunnisett remembers the castle in the war years:

> "We always had the Carnival Dance there in the Rose garden (as it was then) with sand on the slabs to dance on and deck chairs round the edge to sit on. Fairy lights all around and a live band were the order of the day and we all dressed up in pretty dresses. I remember having a long one when I was about eight, I remember these occasions from about 1947 to the early fifties."

Daphne and her daughter-in-law write:

> "Whitstable Castle is a lovely place to visit as it is right by the seafront. It has lovely gardens and the Orange Room where you can get a nice cup of tea with lovely food, with plenty of history to find out as you look over the castle with its many rooms."

Margaret Hunnisett writes:

"At the beginning of the 1950s, my little group of friends, aged around 10 - 12, used Whitstable Castle Grounds as a 'playground'. Yes, in those days it was acceptable and quite safe for children to go off and play for the day. We would take a bottle of water (or squash if we could scrounge it!) a couple of Marmite sandwiches and our parents didn't have to worry about us (well, they probably should have done sometimes!) And the worst that happened to us was perhaps grazed knees or we lost "something"!

The Castle grounds were a great meeting place for several 'gangs' and sometimes it was warfare! But mostly we played happily together.

There was a 'summerhouse' quite near to the Castle which, if you were 'in the know' had two floors. We were 'in the know' and used the top floor as our camp base. We knew we were not supposed to climb up there and whenever a 'grounds person' or other 'annoying adult' appeared, we would lie flat on the upper floor and hoped not to get caught.

Looking back, what happy innocent memories! I wonder what happened to the summer-house? Unfortunately, I do not have any photos.

While at the Endowed school, our art teacher commissioned us (in our own time, of course) to go and study the Castle and then we had to submit paintings of it. My attempt did not get very highly marked, I am afraid, possibly due to the fact that my 'masterpiece' had a matchstick man or woman hanging out of one of the upstairs' windows!

Another memory, when I was 'much older', 14 or 15, my friend's parents used to take us to 'dances' in the Castle grounds in the summertime. I remember thinking how grand it all was with fairy lights in the trees and, I think, the Norman Perkins, band. There were never many boys to dance with but we danced with each other or with the dads! Happy memories!"

CONCLUSION

Whitstable Castle (originally called Tankerton Towers) begun life in 1790 as a summer residence by the sea and is now a valued venue for the community. It sits in an elevated position with views out to sea. It has recently (2008 – 2010) undergone a complete refurbishment of both the castle and surrounding gardens. This was thanks to the £2m Heritage Lottery Grant and funding from Canterbury City Council.

It used to house some of Whitstable Council Offices and was used for playgroups and other community functions.

Every May Bank Holiday, alongside the festivals in the town, it housed a fair where the grounds were full of stalls from local community groups and craft stalls.

Now the old flat-roofed extension has been removed and it has been restored to reflect the era in which it was built. The Orangery tea room serves light lunches and teas and overlooks the beautiful grounds, garden and bowling green – a perfect setting for a summer day.

It is an excellent venue for weddings, parties, local and community events, classes and corporate events.

INDEX

Radford	17-18, 51
Pearson	17-19, 21-22, 25, 28, 41, 51-52, 54-55, 63
Ellis	22-23, 25, 27-29, 41, 52-55
Graystone	26-30, 55, 63
Lloyd	26-29
Robinson	30-32, 35-38, 53, 63
Pinero	39-40
Adams	41, 44
Mallandain	4, 43-46, 54-55, 63